THE ENGAGEMENT

A Comedy
by
RICHARD VETERE

Dramatic Publishing
Woodstock, Illinois • London, England • Melbourne, Australia

*** NOTICE ***

The amateur and stock acting rights to this work are controlled exclusively by THE DRAMATIC PUBLISHING COMPANY without whose permission in writing no performance of it may be given. Royalty fees are given in our current catalog and are subject to change without notice. Royalty must be paid every time a play is performed whether or not it is presented for profit and whether or not admission is charged. A play is performed any time it is acted before an audience. All inquiries concerning amateur and stock rights should be addressed to:

DRAMATIC PUBLISHING
P. O. Box 129, Woodstock, Illinois 60098

COPYRIGHT LAW GIVES THE AUTHOR OR THE AUTHOR'S AGENT THE EXCLUSIVE RIGHT TO MAKE COPIES. This law provides authors with a fair return for their creative efforts. Authors earn their living from the royalties they receive from book sales and from the performance of their work. Conscientious observance of copyright law is not only ethical, it encourages authors to continue their creative work. This work is fully protected by copyright. No alterations, deletions or substitutions may be made in the work without the prior written consent of the publisher. No part of this work may be reproduced or transmitted in any form or by any means, electronic or mechanical, including photocopy, recording, videotape, film, or any information storage and retrieval system, without permission in writing from the publisher. It may not be performed either by professionals or amateurs without payment of royalty. All rights, including but not limited to the professional, motion picture, radio, television, videotape, foreign language, tabloid, recitation, lecturing, publication, and reading are reserved.

SPECIAL NOTE ON SONGS AND RECORDINGS
For performance of any songs and recordings mentioned in this play which are in copyright, the permission of the copyright owners must be obtained or other songs and recordings in the public domain substituted.

©MCMXCVIII by
RICHARD VETERE

Printed in the United States of America
All Rights Reserved
(THE ENGAGEMENT)

Cover design by Susan Carle

ISBN 0-87129-777-9

IMPORTANT BILLING AND CREDIT REQUIREMENTS

All producers of the Play *must* give credit to the Author(s) of the Play in all programs distributed in connection with performances of the Play and in all instances in which the title of the Play appears for purposes of advertising, publicizing or otherwise exploiting the Play and/or a production. The name of the Author(s) *must* also appear on a separate line, on which no other name appears, immediately following the title, and *must* appear in size of type not less than fifty percent the size of the title type. *On all programs this notice should appear:*

"Produced by special arrangement with
THE DRAMATIC PUBLISHING COMPANY of Woodstock, Illinois"

For Lisa Battista, Matt Penn, Randy Finch,
Mary Meagher, Valerie Gordon, Barbara Legiti,
Charlie, Nino, John
and the real inspiration of this play—
my wild, wonderful time in Paris
in the summer of '87.

THE ENGAGEMENT was given its world premiere by the George Street Playhouse in association with Valerie Gordon (Producing Artistic Director Gregory S. Hurst) in New Brunswick, N.J., on September 28, 1991. The cast was as follows:

TOM	Joel Anderson
JEFFERY	Richmond Hoxie
PAT	Michael Countryman
TONY	Joseph Siravo
SUSAN	Melinda Mullins

Director	Matthew Penn
Set Design	Deborah Jasien
Costume Design	Barbara Forbes
Lighting Design	Paul Armstrong
Stage Manager	Thomas Clewell

THE ENGAGEMENT's New York City premiere was given by the Seraphim Theater Company at the Workhouse Theater on June 9, 1995. The cast was as follows:

TOM	Marc Romeo
JEFFERY	Paul Cassell
PAT	Vincent Angell
SUSAN	Rya Kihlstedt
TONY	Andrew Heckler

Director	Randy Finch
Producer	Susan Fried
Set Design	Brad Stokes
Costume Design	Abigail Murray
Stage Manager	Francesca Adair

THE ENGAGEMENT

A Play in Two Acts
For 4 Men and 1 Woman

CHARACTERS

PAT .... assistant college professor, late 20s

JEFFERY .... neighborhood divorce lawyer, late 20s

TOM .... owner of a successful night club, late 20s

SUSAN .... part-time hostess at Tony's restaurant, 20s

TONY .... owner of the family restaurant, 20s

PLACE: New York City.

TIME: The present.

ACT ONE

SCENE ONE

SCENE: *Tony's apartment in New York City. Eight o'clock. The apartment is too slick, too "hip" and downright gaudy with off-the-wall lighting, state-of-the-art stereo equipment and a TV.*

AT RISE: *TOM and JEFFERY pace around the phone, waiting for it to ring as they glance at a cable porn show on the TV screen. The atmosphere is tense and on edge as if they were waiting outside an emergency room. PAT unlocks the door with his key to the apartment and enters the room.*

PAT. Hello, guys...
TOM. Yeah...
JEFFERY. Grab a beer... *(PAT grabs a beer from the refrigerator. As TOM and JEFFERY continue to pace:)*
PAT. So, you guys ready for the Bat Bar?
TOM. We're not going to my club tonight.
PAT. What do you mean? Didn't you call those girls we met the other night? I put on my best jacket! I got a tie on!
JEFFERY. There's been a change of plans.
PAT. Don't tell me that! It's Friday! Hey, I don't want to sit around watching pornos and then wind up sitting in the diner! We always go to the Bat Bar on Friday...

JEFFERY. And Saturday we go to Joey Zane's place, Sunday to the Sports Bar...

TOM. Monday we sleep, Tuesday we eat at Tony's...

JEFFERY. And now, it's the beginning of the end.

PAT. The beginning of what? Hey, by the way, where's Tony?

JEFFERY. He has lost all sense of reality! I can't believe he's going through with it!

PAT. Who?

TOM. We are talking about Tony!

PAT. You know, he has been acting strange. Just last night he had two tickets to the Mets on the field at first base! He tells me he'll meet me there and he never shows! No call, no nothing!

TOM. I love the Mets! I woulda went! Why didn't he call me?

JEFFERY. He should be at her place right now!

PAT. Would you guys tell me what is going on?

TOM. You mean, you don't know? *(To JEFFERY.)* He doesn't know?

JEFFERY. He doesn't know.

PAT. I don't know what? Jeffery left me a message to meet everybody here.

JEFFERY & TOM. Tony's getting engaged!

PAT. To whom?

TOM. Susan!

PAT. Tonight?

JEFFERY. Tonight. *(Pause.)*

PAT. Wow... Why?

JEFFERY. We have no idea.

TOM. He's got to be on drugs! He's got everything—a great business, money! All the women he wants! Why would anyone like that even consider marriage?

Act I THE ENGAGEMENT 11

PAT. Hell, maybe he's in love? *(JEFFERY and TOM stop pacing and stare at PAT. JEFFERY races to the phone.)*
JEFFERY. Love is emasculating. Maybe we should call him?
PAT. Would you guys please tell me what WE are doing here?
JEFFERY. Tony's going to call us from her place. He's going to let us know what happens. He says he needs moral support.
PAT. You mean, she doesn't know?
TOM. WE just found out today! *(PAT, stunned, sits. JEFFERY and TOM pace.)*
PAT. What do we do?
TOM. Tony calls, he's happy, he's in love, HE IS DEAD! *(PAT takes out a paperback book.)*
JEFFERY. You are going to read now?
PAT. At moments of stress, I like taking out a book. You know that. It gives me perspective. *(Shows book.) Wuthering Heights.* I've read it nine times. *(Uneasy.)* For my class.
TOM. We don't need "perspective"! We need a...war! A catastrophe! Something to take his mind off this—disaster!
PAT. Look, he's a grown man. If this is what he wants, it's up to him.
JEFFERY. Look, you and Tony grew up together, right?
PAT. I knew Tony when he was four feet high and four feet wide and getting a pack of bubble gum was the high point of my day.
TOM. Hey, I go back to when Tony and I jumped our first johnny pump without a jock cup.
JEFFERY. Okay, fine, but I meet Pat at Queens College. Through Pat I get to know Tony and you, Tom, and you know what, guys? I have had the best twelve years of

my life! Every summer we rent a house in the Hamptons, in the winter we rent a ski house at Bear Mountain, every four years we go to Europe, we travel to every Super Bowl, we fly to the World Series... I can honestly say that I have friends!

PAT. Okay.

JEFFERY. But I had friends before I met you guys—the guys I grew up with over in Bayside. But who sees them, anymore? They got married! Marriage ruins friendships!

TOM. Ah! Why does a guy ever want to get married, anyway? You know what happens to him once he's there? He's not himself anymore—he's a couple! And then when the kids come, he's got to spend the rest of his life paying bills! He can't buy himself nice clothes! He's got to feed the kids, send them to school, go to P.T.A. meetings! And then his wife stops paying attention to him just like that! Both of my brothers are married and I saw it happen to them. I see that look on their faces when I stop by to say hello. They can't stop talking to me! "Tom! Tom! Talk to me, Tom!" they say. Their kids don't pay attention to them. Their wives don't pay attention to them. They are strangers in their own homes!

JEFFERY. And when a guy talks about marriage he is talking about playing in their home field where they have all the advantages.

PAT. Now, come on, guys. We have all been around a bit... we've dated a lot of women and you know that there is something to be said about having someone special to be there with you... care about you. You're making marriage sound like the last step before death.

TOM. Go ahead, laugh, Professor! But you don't live with a woman! I do. And what I have figured out is that men

Act I THE ENGAGEMENT 13

and women are never talking about the same thing at the same time! Denise is driving me crazy! She walks around the apartment in these little panties. "Hon, let's have some fun," I say to her. "Fun?" she says. "Not even a hooker thinks it's fun!" she says. "And a hooker gets paid for it." So I throw a bill on the bed. "Here! Now can we please have some fun!"

PAT. Interesting love life you and Denise have, Tom.

TOM. You guys remember my father. He was a good guy, right? Quiet, sure, but he did his thing. Well, he used to tell me that if you want a woman you gotta take possession of her. I used to think he was an idiot—but now I know he was right. You walk into a relationship on equal footing and you'll never win! Because women aren't equal to us, they are STRONGER than us! *(Pause.)* Denise is driving me crazy.

JEFFERY *(sadly)*. Poor Tom.

PAT *(looks at TV)*. What are you guys looking at?

TOM. It's a cable porn show.

JEFFERY. Tom knows one of the girls. *(ALL stop and look.)*

PAT. That her?

TOM *(turns his head to see better)*. I think so.

JEFFERY. Can we turn this off?

TOM *(changes channels)*. There's gotta be a movie on...

PAT. Look, maybe we are overreacting.

JEFFERY. Don't tell me! You think I'm overreacting? I'll give you something to overreact to—think about this: almost half of everybody you know who is married today, will wind up getting divorced! And when have you heard of a divorce that was amicable? I'll tell you what I think, I think people get married with stars in their eyes and they get divorced with guns in their hands! And when it's divorce they want that's when they come walking into my office with HATE in their eyes! Hey, pal, I sit through these divorce cases! And it...amazes me! The brutality! The horror! People who held hands like children, people who swore to love each other forever, people who slept in the same bed together night after night, turn into vicious animals! I just finished a case yesterday where I represented this very sweet guy who was suing his wife for divorce after eight years of marriage. He paid me twenty thousand dollars and kept us in court for two years just to stop his wife from getting ownership of a broken-down hassock! When we won, he threw the hassock in the garbage!

PAT. My God.

JEFFERY. And they were childhood sweethearts!

TOM. Hey, I remember this movie. *(ALL look.)*

PAT. Jimmy Stewart... *It's a Wonderful Life.*

JEFFERY. I've seen this... Donna Reed.

PAT. This is the part when he proposes to her. *(ALL watch.)* He wants to leave Bedford Falls but he loves her.

TOM. Yeah, he's in tears.

PAT. He tells her he doesn't want to marry her and have kids and give up all his dreams.

TOM. He's crying.

JEFFERY. Help him.

TOM. The guy is drowning... it's too late! He's hooked!

JEFFERY. Stop him! Jimmy, don't! He's looking into her eyes! Don't look into her eyes!

TOM. Run, pal! Get a drink! Look for your friends! He's thinking how good she feels! Look at him! He's remembering all those nights he had her! The nights she walked around in her panties!

Act I   THE ENGAGEMENT   15

JEFFERY. He's afraid he's going to lose her to somebody else!
TOM. Lose her! *(Pause.)* What am I saying?
JEFFERY. It's a conspiracy, Jimmy! You are not alone! Fight it! Tom, the man needs help!
TOM. You're gonna wind up fat, bald and old before your time!
JEFFERY. Oh, God, stop the man! Please! SOMEBODY STOP HIM! *(Amazed by their reaction, PAT shuts off the TV to stop their agony. The phone rings. Lights out.)*

SCENE TWO

SETTING: *Susan's apartment. The apartment is bohemian-style with books neatly lining one wall and graphic designs lining the other. There is the touch of the artist in the place and, though modest, it is clean and radiates a warmth.*

AT RISE: *SUSAN is in the bedroom offstage as TONY speaks on the phone.*

TONY. Tom, yeah, it's me. Look, don't leave my place. No...everything is fine. Nothing happened yet, I gotta go. Just wait for me there.

(SUSAN enters.)

TONY. What do you mean, you have a date?
SUSAN. Just that: I have a date.

TONY. With who?
SUSAN. Tony!
TONY. I came here to marry you!
SUSAN. Marry me?
TONY. Yeah, look! I have a ring and everything...
SUSAN. You don't call me for three weeks then you pop up and tell me you are going to marry me, just like that?
TONY. Just like that, doll.
SUSAN. And I have nothing to say about it?
TONY. Of course, you have things to say about it.
SUSAN. How's "no"?
TONY. No what?
SUSAN. No, I don't want to marry you, right now. I have a date.
TONY. Hey, what's going on here? I'm your knight in shining armor.
SUSAN. We've been dating for three years, Tony! We've never even talked about marriage until tonight! In all of this time you've kept me close enough for me to care about you, but just far enough to make me feel off balance. These last few weeks, I sat by that phone waiting for you to call, and when you didn't—surprise, surprise—I was able to walk the tightrope on my own! I like my life better without you, Tony—I have balance that way. I don't want a knight in shining armor. And I don't want you. Goodbye. *(TONY is stunned. Lights out.)*

Act I THE ENGAGEMENT 17

SCENE THREE

SETTING: *Tony's apartment. Later that night.*

AT RISE: *TONY walks into his apartment looking confident but obviously anxious at the same time. JEFFERY, TOM and PAT jump to him as he comes through the door. TONY ignores them as he makes himself a drink.*

JEFFERY. So? Tell us! What happened?
TONY. What do you mean, what happened?
TOM. How did it go?
TONY. How did it go?
JEFFERY. Goddamit, Tony! Are you getting married?
TONY. That's what I went over there for, no?
JEFFERY. You picked a date, and everything?
TONY. I was thinking April. April is such a beautiful month.
JEFFERY. I don't believe it. You did it?
TOM. Hey, where's Susan?
TONY. Susan, who?
PAT. Susan! You know, the woman you are going to marry?
TONY. Oh, she's busy.
TOM. I thought you were coming back here with her?
TONY. She couldn't make it.
TOM. Why not?
TONY. She has a date. *(ALL stop and stare at TONY.)*
JEFFERY. Come again?
TONY. Susan, my Susan. She has... *(Breaks down and cries.)*
PAT. Tony, what's the matter?

TONY *(regains composure)*. I'm fine. I'm all right. *(Breaks down again.)*

JEFFERY. Take a deep breath... *(TONY takes a deep breath.)* Now, tell us what happened.

TONY. I got there, you know, with the ring. *(TONY takes out the engagement ring and the GUYS jump back when they see it.)* And I tell her, "Hey, babe, this is for you. I want you to be my blushing bride."

PAT. Poetic.

TONY. Thanks. So, I show her the ring and she tells me, "I can't get married right now, I got a date."

TOM. A date? Like with another guy? *(The GUYS step away from TONY giving him a long look.)*

TONY. Yeah. Jeff, you're smart. What does she mean? You know, "I can't get married right now, I have a date." Hey, I have been around but you know women, they talk in codes. I might be too close to the situation to figure this one out. What is she telling me?

PAT *(deadpan)*. She's telling you she doesn't want to get married right now, she has a date.

JEFFERY. Don't be so hasty, Pat. Women do talk in codes. Tony has got a point here. She said, "I can't get married now," right?

TONY. Right.

TOM. Could mean a number of things.

JEFFERY. What's the next part?

TONY. "I have a date."

TOM. That's pretty clear.

JEFFERY. Is it?

PAT. You guys are a kick! Tony hasn't seen her for a few weeks! I, myself, thought it was over! Obviously, Susan did too. That is what she is telling him.

Act I THE ENGAGEMENT 19

JEFFERY. Are you sure about that, Pat? Think about it.

TONY. You mean, I still have a chance?

JEFFERY. A woman cannot say no to a marriage proposal, Tony. It's genetic.

PAT. Come on, Jeffery, you're being cruel to Tony. It's obviously finished between them.

JEFFERY. You think this thing is over? Not by a long shot, my friend. The negotiations are just beginning.

TOM. It's a power play. She wants you to come back begging. Use your head, Tony.

TONY. What are you guys talking about? I want to get married! I love that girl! Why is she doing this to me?

JEFFERY. She is setting up the parameters of the relationship: master, servant. You have to dump her and move on. It's a stupid impulse, Tony. You'll get over it. We will help you fight it. Consider yourself an addict. *(TONY places the engagement ring on the small table under a bright light. He sits and looks at it forlornly.)*

TOM. A friend gets married and all of a sudden, he starts calling the woman he married his wife, and she starts calling him her husband. When she thinks he's with me, she calls me to ask if I know where he is. She asks, "Have you seen my husband?" I know his name. What happened to his name? I knew you when you both had names!

TONY. "Man and wife," are such beautiful words.

TOM. Tony, listen to me! You're worth big bucks in real estate! You have your restaurant! You can find another lady! You have all the credentials, believe me!

TONY. I want Susan.

PAT. Tom, you are not exactly an enlightened guy, are you?

TOM. Listen, pal, I remember my father sitting in the dark watching TV alone. "I have no friends," he used to say to me. "I'm married forty-one years and I have no friends. Don't let that happen to you," he said to me in the dark. *(To TONY.)* Don't let that happen to you!

TONY. Everything reminds me of her. The photos I have of her hanging over my bed. The clothes she bought me. She bought me this shirt! The cologne I am wearing. She bought me that, too. She helped me pick out the colors for my apartment—both of them. I can't even look at the walls without thinking of her!

PAT. Why did you decide you wanted to get married now?

TONY. Remember when I went to my cousin Louie's wedding last month? Well, right after the dessert and coffee, I was sitting there all by myself and across the room I saw my grandmother and grandpa and my aunt Angie and my uncle Gino and their five kids: my cousins Anthony, Carlino, Frank, Maria and Sal and right next to them was my mother and father, married thirty years! And then I looked around the room and I saw over 250 relatives and it dawned on me—thirty years from now when I'm an old man there won't be anybody in my life to love me!

PAT. So, why'd you wait so long?

TONY. Oh, so it's my fault?

PAT. You didn't call her for three weeks!

TONY. Of course I couldn't call her. You know my situation with Barbara.

PAT. And Carolyn.

TONY. Yeah, Carolyn just left town and Barbara...you KNOW how Barbara can twist me up...

TOM. So with these other ladies why do you care about Susan?

TONY *(walks over to the diamond ring on the table)*. I want Susan to have my children. *(PAT, TOM and JEFFERY cautiously step to the ring.)*

TOM. Horrifying little monster, isn't it?

JEFFERY. My mother wore hers all her life. My sister has one. *(Pause.)* You ever sleep with a girl who's wearing one and you didn't buy it for her?

TOM *(broad smile)*. This chick on Long Island...

TONY. HOW CAN I GO ON LIVING! Every song I hear is cutting right through me! "The Way We Were," "You Lost That Loving Feeling." "Feelings" was our theme song!

PAT. Your relationship had a theme song?

TONY. All my relationships have theme songs. *(TOM, JEFFERY and PAT get interested.)* Sure, Lisa loved "When a Man Loves A Woman." ...Patty's theme song was "Every Breath You Take."

TOM. Spare us.

TONY. And tonight she's out with another guy! Susan! My Susan! I love that woman—and she's on a date! It's killing me!

JEFFERY. Where were they going?

TONY. THEY? THEY? That kills me! THEY! The love of my life on a DATE!

TOM. How long she know this guy?

TONY. I don't...know... Right now they're probably walking down the street...holding hands...

JEFFERY. Maybe they're just having dinner?

TONY. Maybe, he's a cook! He coulda cooked at home... HIS HOME!

JEFFERY. Does she drink wine?

TONY. She LOVES wine...when she drinks her toes curl up...she forgets where she is...we spent a great weekend in the Bahamas...Oh, God...this guy is getting her drunk!

TOM *(checks watch)*. Could be.

JEFFERY. Would she sleep with him?

TONY. Oh, God!

PAT. Not on the first date.

JEFFERY. He doesn't know if it's the first date.

TOM. If they are over thirty and interested you got a 50/50 shot they will sleep with you on the first date. If they are between twenty-six and thirty you got a better shot that they will hold out till the second date. Under twenty-six, unless they are hookers, you could wind up dating the babes for a good two to three weeks before you get the little darlings unwrapped.

JEFFERY. Susan is twenty something...

TOM. Could be first date or second date...I see a 50/50 shot here...

TONY. You think praying will help?

PAT. Fifty/fifty isn't all that bad...

TOM. Yeah, right. You ever hear Vegas give 50/50 odds?

TONY. He'll see her body.

JEFFERY. Some people like it in the dark.

TONY. Her beauty mark near her nipple...

TOM. She does have nice tits...

TONY. And he's going to see them.

PAT. Not all guys are into tits.

JEFFERY. True. I wonder if a woman makes love to different men the same way? Know what I mean?

TOM. Not all guys like the same thing.

PAT. But we are pretty close.

Act I THE ENGAGEMENT 23

JEFFERY. I see Tom's point. For instance...Kim tells me how her husband likes to touch her a certain way...and she doesn't like it when he does it...but when I do it... she loves it...

TONY. Stop it! Stop it! I don't want to think about this guy touching her where I used to touch her!

TOM *(sharply)*. Jeff, you believe that?

JEFFERY. Huh?

TOM. "I don't like it when he does it...but I LOVE it when you do..." Do you believe that?

JEFFERY. Chameleons. They adjust to the man in their life. They make him feel like a million bucks. How can I trust a woman who's unfaithful to her husband with me? I'm a shmuck. You depress me, Tom.

TONY. I can never face my mother again. She loved Susan.

PAT *(waves JEFFERY and TOM over and away from TONY)*. We have to help him.

JEFFERY. What do you suggest?

PAT. He's miserable without her. Let's help them get back together.

TOM. You crazy?

PAT. So, they get together, so what? *(TONY edges his way to his phone and dials.)*

TOM. We will never see him again.

JEFFERY. Wait, Pat has a point. We should confront her.

TOM. You sure you know what you are saying? If Denise ever found out that Tony and Susan were getting married, she will never stop pressuring me! THINK OF YOUR FRIENDS!

PAT. You make it sound like a war, Tom.

TOM. It is! *(The GUYS turn to TONY who holds the phone and cries into it.)*

TONY. She won't answer! *(ALL run to TONY.)* My God! She won't pick up! She's got her machine on!

PAT. Maybe she isn't home...it's only nine o'clock?

TONY. Maybe she is doing it in a cab!

PAT. Tony, stop makin' Susan sound like a sex-crazed animal!

TOM. Yeah, just because you're one!

JEFFERY. Tony, we're going to help you.

TONY. You're gonna have the guy shot!

JEFFERY. No, better...we are going to go to the root of the problem. We will go to Susan and let her know how you feel. We'll see what's on her mind.

TOM. We are?

JEFFERY. Trust me.

TONY. You guys would do that for me?

PAT. You need friends. We're here.

TONY. You guys are great! *(TONY hugs the GUYS. They do a sports-like cheer.)*

TOM, JEFFERY, PAT & TONY. YO!

TONY *(helps himself to a drink)*. When will you talk to her?

JEFFERY. I don't know...maybe tonight after her date...

TONY. Her DATE? Don't say that word around me!

JEFFERY. Sure. You okay now?

TONY *(takes a deep breath)*. Yeah... I'm fine... You guys...my friends will talk to her...great... *(TONY forces a smile then walks to R and stops.)* Do me one favor—all right?

TOM. Anything, pal.

TONY. Don't let her know that I know you guys are doin' this for me.

PAT. Don't let her know you know we are going over there?

Act I   THE ENGAGEMENT   25

TONY. Yeah, you know, tell her what a great guy I am, how much money I make, how much I love her, but her time is limited. You got that. Hey, Tony don't wait around forever for any one chick. You got that?

PAT. You want us to tell her that her time is limited and she better make her mind up how she feels about you immediately?

TONY. Be generous. Give her till tomorrow morning. About ten. Tell her to call me about ten. I will accept her apology after my breakfast.

PAT. Tony, what's the use of us going over there with that attitude? She already said she doesn't want you!

TONY. You're my friends! You said you'd fix it for me!

PAT. What the hell does she see in you? You're nuts!

TONY. I love her!

PAT. No...no...what does she see in YOU?

TONY. I love her.

TOM. Pathetic. Women amaze me the kind of guys they run around with. Tony, if you weren't my friend I'd be sure you were an idiot.

JEFFERY. Tony, go to sleep. We will take care of this... OUR way.

TONY. Jeffery, he's a friend! Jeffery, you're my one true friend.

JEFFERY. Thanks, now go to sleep.

TONY. Susan, the woman of my dreams, goes on a date with a strange guy. My life will never be the same.

TOM. Hey, Tony, take this THING with you. *(TONY picks up the engagement ring off the table. He then solemnly exits clutching it to his heart.)*

TONY *(singing)*. "Feelings...nothing more than feelings..."

TOM. Jeffery, explain this to me: we are going to talk to Susan about Tony?
PAT. Yeah, Jeffery, I am concerned about trusting you.
JEFFERY. Relationships are the courtroom drama of life, and I have passed the bar. Just follow my lead, boys. *(Lights out.)*

SCENE FOUR

SETTING: *Susan's apartment. Hours later.*

AT RISE: *SUSAN enters, puts on the lights, takes off her jacket, when there's a knock at the door.*

SUSAN. Who is it?
JEFFERY *(offstage)*. It's Jeffery.
TOM *(offstage)*. And Tom.
PAT *(offstage)*. And Pat.

(SUSAN opens the door letting JEFFERY, TOM and PAT in.)

SUSAN. Well, hello, this is a surprise.
JEFFERY. It's not too late for you, is it, Sue?
TOM. Hi, Sue.
PAT. Susan.
SUSAN. Hi, Tom...Pat...too late for what?
JEFFERY. To talk.
SUSAN. About?
JEFFERY. Tony.

Act I   THE ENGAGEMENT   27

SUSAN. Oh, Tony...I should have figured that. Is he okay?

TOM. Not really.

SUSAN. Nothing happened to him, did it? I mean, he didn't have an accident or anything like that, did he?

PAT. Nothing like that.

TOM. The man IS suicidal.

SUSAN. He'll survive. Someone with an ego as large as his couldn't dare kill himself.

JEFFERY. That's not what we're worried about, Sue.

PAT. He really LOVES you.

SUSAN. Guys, it's late and I am tired...and I told Tony how I felt about him and HIS plan for us.

JEFFERY. That's the reason why we are here to talk to you. It's about Tony's plans.

SUSAN. I know you guys are his friends...and you are concerned about Tony and everything, but you don't know what I've been through because of him. I want to stay away from him for a while...see other people...live my own life.

JEFFERY. That's fine. We agree with you.

PAT. We do?

JEFFERY. We think it's terrific that you want to stay away from him. If that's what you really mean.

SUSAN. What I really MEAN? Huh?

JEFFERY. Women say those things, Susan. You know that...we know that. It's happened to me before...it's happened to other guys. They tell you... "I don't want to see you anymore..." and Boom! What they really mean is that they want you to CHASE them...go AFTER them... ROMANCE them.

SUSAN. What?!

TOM. What we would like to know is do you mean what you are saying when you tell us that you want to stay away from Tony? Really mean it.

PAT. I'm a little confused here...

SUSAN. What does it matter to you? I don't get the point. Why do you want to know what I mean?

JEFFERY. We want to know if we are on the same side.

SUSAN. Same side?

JEFFERY. You see, Susan, we don't want Tony to see you either.

PAT. Wait a minute...I knew I didn't trust you, Jeffery...

SUSAN. You're telling me, Jeffery...that you...

TOM. Me, too, Sue.

SUSAN. You guys are telling me to stay away from Tony?

PAT. Those guys, not me.

JEFFERY. In so many words.

SUSAN. Why? What's wrong with me? I'm not good enough for your big-shot pal, Tony dumb-nuts!

TOM. No reason to lose your temper, Sue.

JEFFERY. It's not you, Sue, we like you.

TOM. Nicest chick Tony ever went with.

SUSAN. I don't get it? *(In quick succession they say:)*

JEFFERY. It's marriage. We don't want to lose our friend.

TOM. And it will happen.

JEFFERY. There are a lot of nice guys out there.

TOM. Better even.

JEFFERY. Find somebody else.

TOM. Keep our friendship alive with Tony.

JEFFERY. We know him longer. *(Amazed, SUSAN is incredulous and sits. JEFFERY and TOM surround her, with PAT stepping back and watching.)*

PAT. You guys are characters, you really are.

TOM. Hey, let me tell you something—I got my freedom now! I have a place to go when I'm not with Denise! I have my *amigos*! If I say, "Hey, guys, let's go away a couple of days," I don't owe an explanation to anybody! Like the time we went to Mexico for four days and stayed two weeks!

JEFFERY. You see, Susan, guys can take each other's company for what it is—fun! We can just hang out and talk sports, we can talk business, we can go out and break things.

TOM. I don't act the same when the girls are around...I feel DIFFERENT. I got to be careful what I say...what I talk about...I HATE IT.

JEFFERY. Marriage does terrible things to both men and women! You ever see a married couple in the same room with a bunch of other people? Look at them real closely. They have zombie eyes! I see it in a lot of women! It's like they are transfixed by something deep inside them because they know that this guy they married is stuck to them. No matter where she goes, he goes. She has to go home with him, talk to him, and sleep with him. It's why married people are fatter than most other people. Their destinies are over. So, they sedate themselves with food. And remember this, Sue, men only marry because they want younger mothers!

TOM. Save us from zombie eyes!

SUSAN. Wait! Wait a minute! I marry your friend, Tony, and you guys are not going to have anything to do on weekends anymore?

JEFFERY. This is our last shot. Tony goes, we go. The gang is done for. Our friendship is over.

PAT. This is wrong, Jeff. You guys are crazy! Friendship can linger and even grow! Just because people are married doesn't mean their spouses can't be friends.

TOM. Wrong, Professor.

JEFFERY. We are fighting for our souls, Sue.

SUSAN. You people sound like some of those men in the books I read. Do you guys hate women?

TOM. We love 'em.

JEFFERY. We just hate what they do to us. We are weak. We are easily manipulated. If we stick together we can lick this. There is no reason Tony should marry you... or anyone. We can give him the attention, the love, the support. The only thing we can't give him...

TOM. Is the sex.

SUSAN. Oh, well, give him that! Give him that and it won't matter who he falls in love with! Maybe you guys are in love with Tony? Maybe all you guys are in love with each other and you won't face it? *(The GUYS take long looks at one another.)*

TOM. What is she saying?

SUSAN. I am saying that maybe you guys are gay!

TOM. I AM NOT GAY. *(TO JEFFERY.)* I'm not gay, right?

JEFFERY. Of course not. Anyway, it's not the point.

PAT. Nobody here is gay but if they were it would be fine with me.

TOM. Are you sure you're not gay?

JEFFERY. Don't fall into her trap, she is trying to divide and conquer.

TOM. Oh.

SUSAN. You know, you have some balls coming here. You know what I should do? I should call Tony up right now and tell him, yes, I will accept his ring! Yes, I will

Act I   THE ENGAGEMENT   31

marry him! The man does have his good qualities! Why not? At least, I know, he loves me! How does that sound to you, Jeffery? *(SUSAN picks up the phone.)*

JEFFERY. As an attorney, a divorce lawyer, I must tell you now, we will not rest until this affair is SQUASHED ... and I know how to break people up ... I do it for a living, Sue. And I have a file on you and Tony ...

TOM. We'll stop at nothing to break you guys up.

PAT. But they broke up?

JEFFERY. I don't believe her.

SUSAN. Wait a minute. You said a file?

PAT. A file?

TOM. A file?

JEFFERY. A file. *(JEFFERY takes a file out of his briefcase.)*

PAT. Holy shit.

SUSAN. On what?!

JEFFERY. Names, dates, matters of interest concerning Susan Ventura and Tony Vendome.

SUSAN *(slowly approaches the file but doesn't touch it)*. You have things about my past in there?

JEFFERY. Your past and Tony's past.

PAT. You are low, Jeffery. Real LOW. What the hell is wrong with you?

SUSAN. Does Tony know about this?

PAT. He thinks we are here to salvage your relationship, not destroy what's left of it.

SUSAN. Has he seen this?

JEFFERY. No, and he doesn't have to. It will be kept in a safe until you are safely away from Tony ... then it will be burned.

PAT. Safely away?

JEFFERY. Three years. As friends, that's all we want.

SUSAN. I stop seeing Tony for three years and you'll bury this...junk?

JEFFERY. Yes. But if you decided to allow him to marry you...we'll read the contents to him...and we will allow you to learn facts about Tony you might rather not know.

SUSAN. I don't want to know about Tony. And I'll kill you if you tell him things about me he has no right knowing!

JEFFERY. Kill me. He marries you and I'm just as dead.

TOM. Boy, we're getting carried away here a little, aren't we, Jeff?

JEFFERY. It's ugly, but it's the way it happens all the time—the way friends drift...the things left unsaid and unspoken...for years. Men allow their friendships to disappear and now, with the world as it is, all male friendships are suspect. We are fighting for the last of the breed. We have to pull out all the punches. I saw this coming. I got the file together a couple of months ago when I saw you two getting close...

SUSAN. We were.

JEFFERY. But something happened?

SUSAN. Something happened.

JEFFERY. It gave me extra time.

PAT. I got a question, Jeff. Do you have a file on me? *(Everyone focuses on TOM when he laughs.)*

TOM *(laughs)*. You got a file on Pat? *(Stops laughing.)* You got a file on ME?

PAT. You got a file on all of us, don't you, Jeffery?

JEFFERY. Yes. I have a file on all of you.

PAT. You dog.

Act I THE ENGAGEMENT 33

TOM. You got a file on me? If Denise ever sees that I'll throw you out of a moving subway car!

JEFFERY. Relax...relax...I got a file on myself...too.

PAT. We'll I'll be...

JEFFERY. As a friend, Pat...Tom...and if Tony were here...I'd make him swear to show it to the woman I was going to marry... *(JEFFERY takes out his file.)* We all have secrets we want to keep from our lovers...Yes, that fact is untrue to what we think true love is...but it is a fact. These secrets we keep to ourselves...keep the peace allowing our relationships to grow...relationships are so fragile they need all the help they can get...so we keep secrets. I've kept this file on myself to keep myself on track...in check. It keeps me intact...whole...free. I have all my sins in this file and whoever gets to love me too much...I can show it to them. This file keeps me safe from losing who I am! I am free from forgetting that I am not perfect, that I am not loving, that I am a selfish creep! I am not some fantasy some woman judges me to be! I am Jeffery! Scared, tainted, and only interested in surviving! I don't deserve to be loved! And that makes me happy! So happy to spend the time of my life on ME! Me!

TOM. Jeff, you don't have the time in my club when those two teenagers took me into the ladies room?

JEFFERY. Oh, that's in there, Tom.

TOM. But not the time the IRS...?

JEFFERY. Page 20...

TOM. Page 20! You got twenty pages in there!

JEFFERY. More than that. I did not skimp. *(TOM quickly picks up his file.)* What will it be, Susan?

SUSAN *(with curiosity)*. Give me that. I want to read it.

JEFFERY. Do you want Tony to do that? Read your life as if it were an open book?

SUSAN. Tony is his own person...so am I.

JEFFERY. In theory.

SUSAN. There is nothing in the file I am ashamed of. *(Suddenly, SUSAN rushes over to her file, picks it up hesitantly, then quickly sits and reads it. The GUYS watch her with intense interest. As she reads, they try to read over her shoulder but SUSAN hugs the file keeping it from their eyes and the lights go down and out.)*

SCENE FIVE

SETTING: *Susan's apartment. Ten minutes later.*

AT RISE: *SUSAN, TOM, JEFFERY and PAT are reading their files.*

TOM *(laughing)*. I don't believe I did this! Wow! What a character I am... You know, I can't complain about my life. I just about screwed every woman I liked...made money when I had to...cheated when I had to...lied when I had to... I could die tomorrow and I think I can say that I lived a satisfying life.

JEFFERY. But would you want Denise to know those things about you?

TOM. This is private, man...this is for me...this is all my good times for posterity.

PAT. You really outdid yourself, Jeff...but I wouldn't mind who read this.

Act I THE ENGAGEMENT 35

JEFFERY. Your life was pretty bland, Pat...assistant professor...only one affair with one student.

PAT. I learned my lesson after that.

SUSAN *(gets up and places her file down on the table)*. I want you out of my apartment, Jeffery... I want all of you out. You had no right to record this...stuff...

JEFFERY. Okay, I will go. But Tony gets a copy of that if you decide to continue seeing him. This is war! Good night.

PAT. Don't count me in on this, Sue.

SUSAN. I won't.

TONY *(offstage)*. I know you're up! I see the lights on! Sue, open up!

SUSAN. Oh, damn...

(SUSAN opens the door and TONY barges in.)

TONY. Where is he?

SUSAN. Where's who?

TONY. The guy you went out with?

SUSAN. He's home. Tony, what are you doing here?

TONY. I came here to kill him.

PAT. You are supposed to stay home.

TONY. How could I stay home when my future wife is seeing somebody else! Did you talk to her for me?

PAT. We tried.

SUSAN. Wonderful friends you have, Tony. Real concerned about you. You know why they came here?

JEFFERY. Susan?

SUSAN. Don't threaten me, Jeffery.

TONY. Hey, what's going on here?

TOM. It's all for your own good.

SUSAN. Your friends came here tonight to save you from marrying me. To stop you from marrying me!

TONY. I don't understand? I'm in love with my Susie. I thought you guys were my friends?

JEFFERY. We are. We are also concerned about ourselves and your friendship with us.

TONY. Huh?

PAT. Jeffery doesn't believe we guys will remain friends once you two are married.

SUSAN. But we're not getting married!

TONY. Don't depress me!

TOM. You aren't listening, Tony, she doesn't want you.

TONY. Shut up, Tom...I don't care if she wants me or not... I love her.

PAT. Good luck, Jeff...

JEFFERY. I *am* your attorney, am I not, Tony?

TONY. Yeah, so?

JEFFERY. As your attorney I believe there are some things about Susan you should know before you tie the knot.

TONY. What things?

SUSAN. Show him that file and I will never talk to you again, Jeffery.

JEFFERY. Marry Tony and I'll probably never hear from either of you again anyway, so I'll take the chance. *(JEFFERY picks up SUSAN's file.)*

PAT. I should stop you from doing this simply on moral grounds.

SUSAN. No, let him. I made up my mind that I'm not in love with Tony anymore and that I have no reason why I should marry him. *(To TONY.)* I'm sorry, Tony, you just burnt me out.

TONY. I'm going to be sick...

Act I   THE ENGAGEMENT   37

JEFFERY. Here, read this...you'll feel better... *(JEFFERY hands SUSAN's file to TONY. He then hands TONY's file to SUSAN.)* What's fair is fair...

TONY. What is this? It's not from the Board of Health about my violations, is it? It's bad enough my restaurant gets printed up in the papers for having a dirty kitchen, you gotta keep a file?

JEFFERY. In these files I had my research team at work compile a list of dates, names and events you have experienced...most of them secret...which have to do with your love life...financial life. Facts, Tony, facts you do not know about Susan...nor does she know about you. It is a file I put together on all of us. Read on, Tony.

TONY. This a joke? You're telling me that you kept a file on me? You crazy? *(Whispers.)* What happens if the government gets this?

JEFFERY. It is only for the eyes of your possible wife-to-be. You don't have to look at any of it...that choice is up to you.

SUSAN. I want you to read it, Tony. I do.

TONY. Sue, what the hell can you be hiding from me? Since that first day you walked into my restaurant with your hair tied back, wearing those funny-colored socks and carrying that knapsack, you were everything I ever dreamed of in a woman.

SUSAN. You remember all that?

TONY *(sweetly)*. As if it happened yesterday.

SUSAN *(slowly)*. But Tony, people change...they grow apart...

TONY. Never you and me.

SUSAN *(frustrated)*. Open it. Read.

PAT. I think it's time for us to get out of here...

SUSAN. No, stay.

TOM. I don't want to miss this.

TONY *(takes the file, proudly, and stands)*. Susan has nothing to hide from me. Jeffery, you'll regret this. Monday I am hiring a new attorney. *(TONY reads. He stops.)* You took acting classes for two years?

SUSAN. I told you that a hundred times. I wanted to be Bette Davis.

TONY *(reads on)*. You're a...graphic artist?! What does that mean? You're naked?

SUSAN. I design textbook covers, dummy! It's what I do since I left the restaurant! You know, nothing stays in that hard head of yours unless it has to do with YOU!

TONY *(reads)*. You were engaged once? You never told me that.

SUSAN. I wanted to.

TONY. Who was he?

SUSAN. Richie Volpe from Springfield Gardens. He was older...

TONY. Why didn't you marry him?

SUSAN. I didn't want to be tied down. I wanted to travel first. He married somebody else. We used to talk, but we don't anymore.

TONY *(reads then puts down the file)*. You were pregnant. You had a miscarriage with this guy. Why didn't you tell me?

SUSAN. I never told you because it didn't matter between us...

TONY. Did you love him?

SUSAN. I did...very much. Once.

TONY. More than you love me?

SUSAN. I don't know what I feel about you, Tony.

Act I THE ENGAGEMENT 39

TONY. Is he better than me or something? What was the difference? What did he look like? He had money, I bet...

SUSAN. It's not important, Tony. Not at all.

TONY *(sulking)*. So, it's no big deal that I asked you to marry me. Hell, somebody asked you first.

SUSAN. I wasn't born the day you met me.

JEFFERY *(to TOM)*. I think it's working...

SUSAN. Screw you, Jeffery! Tony, you don't care if you're second or twenty-second when it comes to me. It's your ego that can't swallow the fact that I don't fall over you like other women!

TONY *(reads)*. You lived with a cowboy from Jersey? Jersey?

SUSAN. They have cowboys in Jersey! He did the rodeo. Steve was a nice guy... I am not embarrassed about my... love life.

TONY. Who is Alan Pulski?

SUSAN. I met him in Europe and we traveled together... I lived with him in Holland for a little while... I told you about him!

TONY. How many guys you sleep with before me?

SUSAN *(pause)*. Nine!

TONY. *Madone!* Nine?! Nine? Nine guys... Nine? You mean, like seven, eight, nine? Nine DIFFERENT guys?

JEFFERY. I thought it read eight?

SUSAN *(sarcastically)*. You missed one.

TONY. This is awful... this is awful to read all this... Jeffery, you suck... you do. *(SUSAN picks up TONY's file.)*

JEFFERY. Maybe we better leave now?

SUSAN. You leave and I will pull out your tongue!

TONY. Yeah, creep, I ain't done with you.

SUSAN *(reading)*. Judge my life, Tony? Okay, Mister Perfect, let's see about yours...

TONY *(falsely)*. I am proud of everything I've ever done.

SUSAN *(reads)*. You make that much money? You told me you were just getting by...I didn't believe it...but you make that much...you OWN that much...?

TONY. Jeffery, I will kill you...

SUSAN. Who is Coral Blue?

TONY *(slowly)*. Coral? She was a...dancer...she slept with a lot of guys...I told her no way that was my kid! *(The GUYS snicker among themselves.)*

SUSAN *(hurt)*. You spent a weekend with Clare...my best friend, Clare? Tony? *(The GUYS are suddenly stunned.)*

TONY. Nothing happened. I swear! We slept in different rooms in the house...Believe me, Susan...PLEASE! I am innocent on that one!

SUSAN. Why didn't you tell me? You lied. You said you spent the weekend with the boys?

TOM. You and Clare?

SUSAN. You liked her, Tony. You always did.

TONY. How could I like her, she was your best friend?

SUSAN. You liked her and you wanted to sleep with her.

TONY. It was just a thought that entered my head.

SUSAN *(to JEFFERY)*. Your plan worked. I liked you better, Tony, when I didn't know everything about you. Jeffery, Tom... I hope I never see the two of you again. Pat, good night... *(She hands her file to JEFFERY.)*

PAT. Good night, Sue...

TOM. Good night...

JEFFERY. Good night...

SUSAN. Get out!

Act I   THE ENGAGEMENT   41

(Lights quickly come down on SUSAN and up on the FOUR GUYS sitting on the curb around a lamppost.)

TONY. I can't believe it's this hard to get married! I mean, when my father wanted to get married, he got down on his knees, said to my Mom, "Angela, I love you. Marry me." And that was it.

PAT. Sure, he didn't have MTV, the swimwear issue of *Sports Illustrated*, Watergate and "Baywatch"—inside his brain.

JEFFERY. You don't need marriage, Tony. You have friends and we'll be friends all our lives.

PAT. Friends, Jeffery? What are friends? If what you did just now is what a friend does, Tony doesn't need friends...

JEFFERY. I did it for you, too. You just don't see it, yet.

TONY. Leave Jeffery alone. I'm glad I found out those things about Susan. I thought she was a nice girl.

PAT. Don't pigeonhole anybody like that, Tony. Susan is just like you: she's trying to make sense out of things that don't make much sense.

TONY. But could you imagine if I married a girl who slept with NINE guys?

PAT. Yeah, you, the pillar of the community.

JEFFERY. It's funny how my research team missed that extra one...

TONY. The world stinks. There's too much money around.

PAT *(sarcastically)*. And all the wrong people have it.

TOM. You know, it's funny. I make more money from my club than my father did in a lifetime working down at the Seagrams factory. Before he died, he came to the opening night of my club and saw all these teenagers standing in line waiting to get in and he turned to me and said, "I don't get it." You know something? He's right, I don't get it either.

TONY. That's true. You and me never went to college and the professor here, who's read more books than Simon Schuster, or whatever his name is, is always broke.

PAT. An educated mind is not necessarily a happy one.

JEFFERY. I went to college.

PAT. You're a lawyer, it doesn't count.

TOM. Hey, it's still early. Let's go to Scores and watch some go-go dancers.

JEFFERY. Good idea. It'll get Tony's mind off Susan.

TONY. I can't look at naked women now, it'll be too painful.

JEFFERY. You have to get Susan out of your mind.

TONY. You are right. I hope that she finds some guy who loves her more than I could. I hope she has a good life.

TOM. So, where to?

TONY. The river! I want to throw myself in!

TOM. Get hold of yourself, Tony!

TONY *(to JEFFERY)*. Is it wrong to love a woman so much? So deeply?

JEFFERY. If you want to keep your sanity, the answer is yes!

TONY *(takes out his cellular phone)*. I should call Susan, you know, say goodbye.

TOM. You said goodbye.

TONY. No, I mean, a real goodbye...a farewell forever. *Au revoir!*

JEFFERY. She wants to sleep. We are taking you out for a drink!

TONY. But I should tell her a romantic "so long" for all the years we spent together! *(TOM and JEFFERY grab TONY who struggles with them.)*

JEFFERY. Tony! I know men still saying goodbye to their ex-wives five years after the divorce when she is already re-married, lives in another country, speaks a foreign language and has three new kids! Cut the ties now! It's less painful in the long run!

TONY *(hands the phone to PAT)*. Help me! Pat! Pat, call her for me! Tell her I will always think of her! I will always love her! Pat!

PAT. I can't call her, Tony! You call her! You call her! *(PAT watches as TONY is dragged offstage by JEFFERY and TOM. They exit. PAT holds the phone not knowing what to do. He waits a few beats then dials. Into phone:)* Susan, it's me. Are you okay? You can't sleep? I know I won't be able to either. Yeah, sure. *(A beat.)* I'll be right over. *(Lights out.)*

END OF ACT ONE

ACT TWO

SCENE ONE

SETTING: *Susan's apartment. Fifteen minutes later.*

AT RISE: *PAT is examining the bookshelf.*

PAT *(in awe).* You have Graham Greene's *The End of the Affair*?

(SUSAN enters with two cups of tea. She places PAT's cup on the table near the sofa and sits. PAT is very tentative. It is clear there is an enormous attraction here and he is trying to stay away from it. SUSAN is more in control.)

SUSAN. One of my top ten favorite love stories.
PAT. I love *Jane Eyre*.
SUSAN. The book?
PAT. The movie with Orson Welles. What's your favorite film?
SUSAN. *Splendor in the Grass*.
PAT. Oh, man! Kill me right here! *(PAT sits on the sofa, realizes what he's done, then stiffens just a little.)*
SUSAN. The last scene?
PAT. It ruined me!
SUSAN. I know. The way Warren Beatty and Natalie Wood were still so desperately in love but they were either married or engaged to other people.

SUSAN. Okay, I am fond of him. And I know that despite his other women he loves me. He adores me. But there is something missing.

PAT. I know what that is. It's a deep, soul-wrenching passion. It's an overwhelming pull deep into another person that makes you forget who you are, where you are...

SUSAN. Yes. Yes. The kind of feeling I had with you.

PAT. And I had with you. *(Pause. They are suddenly being seduced by one another without even realizing it.)*

SUSAN. That night under the stars in your sleeping bag... the moon was a sliver of silver light. And yet as dark as it was I saw you everywhere.

PAT. Your voice... your body in the night. In my arms. I remember, Sue. I remember every night I close out the lights and sleep alone. I even remember nights when I don't sleep alone.

SUSAN. If you remembered, you never told me.

PAT. I know.

SUSAN. You never called when we got back to the city.

PAT. I know.

SUSAN. I felt like trash...

PAT. I felt the same way. We all went on that camping trip to have fun! And Tony leaves me up there with you while he and Tom and Jeffery went to town and didn't come back until Sunday!

SUSAN. Why did they go? To look for girls?

PAT. Yeah.

SUSAN. I figured that. It doesn't matter now. Look what happened!

PAT. Tell me about it.

SUSAN. You were Tony's best friend! Who knew this would happen? And then, what was worse, was that you

Act II   THE ENGAGEMENT   45

PAT. You know, I think for all great love stories to work, the lovers have to part forever at the end of the story, like in *Brief Encounter*...

SUSAN. Or *On the Beach*... Lionel Trilling says that in contemporary times, we love in the face of death.

PAT *(losing control)*. You read Trilling, too?

SUSAN. Second shelf.

PAT. I didn't know that. *(Moves gently away.)* Tony is a good guy.

SUSAN. He's a liar, a cheat, a crook, probably, and a coward.

PAT. No different than most of us.

SUSAN. Why are you defending Tony?

PAT *(stands)*. He's my friend. He loves you. You make him happy.

SUSAN. And what does he do for me?

PAT. I don't know. *You* went out with him for three years.

SUSAN. He's a habit...a routine...

PAT. All the things a relationship is.

SUSAN. The day I met him I was just back from wandering all over the world. I came home. I felt really alone. But when I met him that day, he made me laugh. He helped find this apartment. He knew a guy, who knew a guy, who owns the building. And I really liked his folks and stuff like that but now, I realize, I need MORE.

PAT. More?

SUSAN. I want somebody who knows that there is a world going on beyond Queens! I want somebody who will teach his kids more then just baseball and where to find the local bookie!

PAT. Come on, be honest with yourself. The man makes a lot of money! He owns cars! He even got his mother a job!

TONY. But I should tell her a romantic "so long" for all the years we spent together! *(TOM and JEFFERY grab TONY who struggles with them.)*

JEFFERY. Tony! I know men still saying goodbye to their ex-wives five years after the divorce when she is already re-married, lives in another country, speaks a foreign language and has three new kids! Cut the ties now! It's less painful in the long run!

TONY *(hands the phone to PAT)*. Help me! Pat! Pat, call her for me! Tell her I will always think of her! I will always love her! Pat!

PAT. I can't call her, Tony! You call her! You call her! *(PAT watches as TONY is dragged offstage by JEFFERY and TOM. They exit. PAT holds the phone not knowing what to do. He waits a few beats then dials. Into phone:)* Susan, it's me. Are you okay? You can't sleep? I know I won't be able to either. Yeah, sure. *(A beat.)* I'll be right over. *(Lights out.)*

END OF ACT ONE

ACT TWO

SCENE ONE

SETTING: *Susan's apartment. Fifteen minutes later.*

AT RISE: *PAT is examining the bookshelf.*

PAT *(in awe).* You have Graham Greene's *The End of the Affair*?

(SUSAN enters with two cups of tea. She places PAT's cup on the table near the sofa and sits. PAT is very tentative. It is clear there is an enormous attraction here and he is trying to stay away from it. SUSAN is more in control.)

SUSAN. One of my top ten favorite love stories.
PAT. I love *Jane Eyre*.
SUSAN. The book?
PAT. The movie with Orson Welles. What's your favorite film?
SUSAN. *Splendor in the Grass.*
PAT. Oh, man! Kill me right here! *(PAT sits on the sofa, realizes what he's done, then stiffens just a little.)*
SUSAN. The last scene?
PAT. It ruined me!
SUSAN. I know. The way Warren Beatty and Natalie Wood were still so desperately in love but they were either married or engaged to other people.

avoided me for months after that. You were waiting for the feelings to die out, right?

PAT. I was.

SUSAN. Afraid I'd get serious? *(PAT is silent.)* That's it, isn't it?

PAT. Sue, I have been in love before, a girl named Jackie, you never met her. It was a long time ago. She lived in Ridgewood over on Hart Street. We went out together for nearly five years. It was a time in my life when I was so confused on what I wanted to do with myself. And she wanted to settle down but I looked around my neighborhood and nobody married looked happy. There were always bills to pay, and in my own house there were arguments, accusations, fears of age and time passing too quickly. So, though I loved her, she went on with her life and I went on with mine... and she married somebody else. Sure, I think about her, but where did being in love get me? It left me with, what? Some fond memories?

SUSAN. Maybe it wasn't the right time for you.

PAT. I don't like myself when I feel things for someone. I act like a dope. I wasn't looking for passion or the demands passion makes when you and I—look at Tony! Because of you, he can't sleep, he can't eat, he's ready to change his whole life for you!

SUSAN. And that scares you?

PAT. Yes!

SUSAN. Why? I'm not a monster.

PAT. I am afraid of desire. I am afraid of someone else running my life because I desire them. Because I need them. And worst of all, Susan, my dear—giving, vulnerable Susan—I am afraid of being STUCK with that person way after the desire for them dies.

SUSAN. What do you want?

PAT. A friend. It's all I want from anyone. My passion for you, for anyone, is going to be too demanding of me.

SUSAN. Friends can be too demanding, too. It demands giving of yourself even when you get nothing in return.

PAT. Then be my friend! *(A loud bang at the door.)*

TONY *(offstage)*. I see the lights on! Let me in!

SUSAN *(goes to the door)*. Darn him!

(SUSAN opens the door and TONY races in.)

SUSAN. Go away, Tony!

TONY. Pat! Glad you're here! I thought that guy she went out with came back.

PAT. Where are the guys?

TONY *(gleefully)*. I dodged them at the China Club! I went to the bathroom and snuck out the back way! *(To SUSAN.)* I came here to say goodbye to you... I came here to tell you that I wish you all the happiness in the world!

SUSAN. You could have waited till tomorrow. I'm not going anywhere.

TONY. I might be dead tomorrow. I want you to know I am considering suicide! It's true! I have no reason to live if you won't have me! My life will be a mistake if you don't marry me! Without you, I have nothing! *(TONY grabs a bottle of Scotch and pours himself a strong drink.)*

SUSAN. I don't want to hear that, Tony.

TONY. It's the way I feel. I am a man of deep feelings. When I feel something, it doesn't go away.

Act II THE ENGAGEMENT

SUSAN. Tony, I have to tell you something...

PAT. I should leave...

SUSAN. It's up to you. Either way, I'm telling him. It'll bring him to his senses. Tony, there is someone else in my life. Someone else... WAS in my life... is better.

TONY. Somebody else? What do you mean? I read the file?

SUSAN. He wasn't in the file. *(PAT makes a move to leave struggling within himself to stay or go.)*

TONY. Somebody else you have feelings for?

SUSAN. That's it. I still have feelings for this person.

TONY. I hate it when women tell you they got feelings for somebody else. They say "I have feelings for someone else" but they don't tell you who! It's mean, it's not fair, they want you to beg! *(TONY gets on his knees in front of SUSAN.)* WHO is he? Tell me and I'll kill him.

PAT. This is sadistic, Sue.

TONY. Thanks, Pat, the whole thing is unfair, it's cruel, it's ugly...

SUSAN. It's Pat. *(Pause.)*

TONY. Pat, who? *(Pause.)*

PAT. It's me, Tony. Your friend. It's me, Susan is talking about.

TONY. My Susan has feelings for you?

SUSAN. I have.

TONY. But feelings mean sex... you know, SEX.

SUSAN. They do.

PAT. I'm sorry, Tony.

TONY. This just happen tonight?

PAT. No, a few months ago.

(JEFFERY and TOM bang on the door, finding it open, they rush in.)

JEFFERY. I knew you'd be here!

TOM. Tony, trust us! Don't run away from us! We're you're friends!

TONY. Your file stinks, Jeffery! You missed Pat! My friend Pat!

JEFFERY. Pat what?

TONY. Pat had an AFFAIR with Susan! *(TONY pours himself another stiff shot and knocks it down.)*

TOM. Come again...

SUSAN. I want everybody out! Okay! This is my house and I want you all out of here!

TONY. Except for Pat, right? Except for you and Pat!

SUSAN. Enough, Tony!

JEFFERY. You mean, Pat and Susan? That was number NINE?

SUSAN. Jeffery, I hope you like death.

JEFFERY. Wait a minute! Are we going to lose Pat to you? Oh, my God, no! Impossible. Noncommittal Pat? The fence sitter? You aren't going down for the count, are you, Pat?

TONY. I'll fight you for her!

PAT. What?

TONY *(takes off his jacket)*. I will fight you for my Susie! You and me, pal!

PAT. You're crazy! I'm not fighting you.

TONY. You and me.

JEFFERY. You're going to fight for her when she slept with your...friend?

Act II   THE ENGAGEMENT   51

TONY. I don't care. I love this woman. I love her more then I did before.

SUSAN. Oh, Tony...

TOM *(to PAT)*. How did it happen? How did you manage to get her when I...

SUSAN. Tom?

TONY. You what?

TOM. Come on, Sue...what turned you on about Pat? I mean, come on, I'm better looking?

TONY. Good question, Tom, you low-life pervert! I'll break your neck later. Susan, answer the man's question.

SUSAN. Why should I?

JEFFERY. I believe Tom has the right to know why you would sleep with one of Tony's friends and not the other!

SUSAN. You sick bastards! Out of my apartment!

TOM. Because Pat's got brains! That's it! Women always go for the guys with brains!

SUSAN. Tom, you have the I.Q. of a spoon!

TOM. I just find it difficult to accept a woman passing me up.

PAT. Hey, Tom, you want to shut up?

TOM. Hey, pal, don't rub me the wrong way.

PAT. It's between me and Susan and that means PRIVATE.

TOM. How about I put you in a headlock and make you talk?

PAT *(gets ready to fight with TOM)*. Anytime...moose face!

TOM. Moose face? *(TOM and PAT circle each other.)*

TONY. Wait! You can't fight him! I'm fighting him!

TOM. After me!

TONY. He slept with my future wife!

SUSAN. I am not marrying you!

TOM. But he did it without telling us! So I should kill him!
JEFFERY. He's not a loyal friend.
PAT. What did you say, Jeffery?
JEFFERY. You are not a loyal friend. *(PAT steps over to JEFFERY and punches him once in the stomach. JEFFERY holds his belly, and falls onto the sofa.)*
TOM. You hit Jeffery?
TONY. He did.
TOM. He's a lawyer? You can't hit a lawyer?
PAT. I can hit whoever I want...and next, I hit you, Tom... *(PAT takes a swing hitting TOM in the gut. TOM holds his stomach, looks incredulously at PAT, then falls onto the sofa next to JEFFERY.)*
TONY. You hit Tom!
PAT. The bigger they are the harder they fall. I learned that in my boxing classes...not bad for my second year.
TONY. You gonna hit me, now?
PAT. No, I am not going to hit you, Tony.
TONY. Okay, but I am going to hit you... *(TONY swings and hits PAT in the stomach. PAT holds his stomach and sits down in the chair.)*
SUSAN. Tony!
TONY. I learned that in the street! Sleep with my girl, that's one thing, but hit my friends, that's another!
SUSAN. I'm calling the police!
TONY. Call 'em! I'll hit them, too! I'll die in a hail of police bullets for my one true love!
SUSAN. Tony, listen to me...calm down...listen to me.
TONY. I'm calm... I am... I'm calm.
SUSAN. I do love you. But I'm not IN love with you!
TONY *(in pain, stumbles around)*. No! Not that one! No, please! I could take the one where you have feelings for

Act II — THE ENGAGEMENT — 53

some other guy, but not the one where you love me but you're not IN love with me... Oh, God... I can't take it anymore... *(TONY is suddenly motionless, makes an UGH! sound, then closes his eyes and falls to the floor, unconscious.)*

SUSAN. Tony?

JEFFERY. He's out.

TOM. It's all the booze. He's allergic to it. He gets a bad reaction.

PAT. He'll have to sleep it off.

SUSAN. Terrific... I never saw this before...

JEFFERY. He gets embarrassed about it and doesn't want anybody to know.

TOM. So he only gets drunk around his friends. *(The GUYS pick TONY up and place him on the sofa. PAT opens JEFF's file. SUSAN, depressed, sits on a chair C and looks out at the audience.)*

SUSAN. My life was beginning to make sense before tonight. I had gotten Tony nearly out of my mind... I told myself Pat never felt a thing for me... and now Tony is asleep on my couch begging me to marry him... and Pat tells me he had PASSION for me. My life has suddenly gotten complicated all because of you, Jeffery.

JEFFERY. I'm a lawyer.

SUSAN. You are going to wish you and your damn file never existed!

JEFFERY. It's getting late.

SUSAN *(stands in front of the door blocking JEFFERY's escape)*. Listen up, guys, there is something I want Jeffery to hear! This married woman he's been seeing? Kim? We had lunch.

JEFFERY. Susan, you're blocking my way...

SUSAN. We met a few months ago at Tom's birthday party at Tony's, and just the other day we bumped into each other shopping.

JEFFERY. Come on, Susan, give me the file.

SUSAN. She is very pretty... lovely, warm.

PAT. Nice lady.

SUSAN. I hope what I tell you DEVASTATES you, Jeffery...

TOM. You got some juicy stuff to tell us? Is it in the file?

SUSAN. No, you won't find what I have to say in the file.

JEFFERY. I don't want to hear it!

SUSAN. I hope what I tell you haunts you to your dying day...

JEFFERY. Someone help me!

SUSAN. Oh, Jeffery, what Kim had to tell me is going to squash you. It's going to rock your world...

JEFFERY. Please, don't tell me, Sue...

SUSAN. Kim's been married for seven years... has two little girls: Tracy and Dawn. She comes from a nice family in Boston.

JEFFERY. Please... please...

SUSAN. Her husband is a wonderful man! Works for the Pentagon... as an attorney... he's devoted, caring and supportive...

JEFFERY. STOP!

TOM. Gee, Jeff, she hasn't said anything yet...

SUSAN. Haven't I? This women has a perfect life! She has everything she's ever dreamed of, but guess what?

TOM. What?

SUSAN. Guess what is the worse thing that ever could happen to her!

TOM. I don't know...

JEFFERY. Stop!

SUSAN. You know what I'm going to say, don't you, Jeffery?

Act II   THE ENGAGEMENT

TOM. She caught herpes from him?

SUSAN. Worse!

PAT. She got pregnant?

SUSAN. Worse!

TOM. She caught something and she doesn't know WHAT it is?

SUSAN. Worse!

PAT. She has three weeks to live?

SUSAN. Worse! SHE FELL IN LOVE WITH HIM! *(Pause.)*

JEFFERY *(in pain)*. Awwhhhh!

TOM. Is that possible?

JEFFERY. Awwhhhh!

PAT. Incredible...

TOM. She loves Jeffery? How could anybody love Jeffery?

SUSAN. She loves him more then his own mother could!

PAT. No one can love a son more than his own mother!

SUSAN. I had lunch with the woman! I know!

TOM. Wow. I never thought it was as bad as all this... I figured she was just some married chick he was doing on the side.

SUSAN. She loves you, Jeffery... she sat all through lunch in tears... not knowing what to do... she never felt the way she does for any man... not even her husband... A woman loves you, Jeffery! And what are you going to do about it? Tell us!

JEFFERY *(stunned)*. Ahhhhhh!

PAT *(holding up JEFFERY's file)*. Jeff, you want me to show this to Kim?

JEFFERY *(grabbing file)*. Give me that!

SUSAN. She believes he is a compassionate saint!

PAT. Love is blind.

JEFFERY. Being loved is to live... with such an awful burden... I feel weak... I feel like I should go home...
SUSAN. Call her and show her the file... that might help change her mind... her feelings...
TOM. Jeff, get strong, pal...
JEFFERY. I'll show her the file.
TOM. That's the spirit. Let's get back to Tony's and we will talk this out.
JEFFERY. Take me to Tony's. I don't want to go home. I don't trust myself alone tonight. Please.
TOM. Oh, buddy, oh, pal... don't worry about nothing. Sue, 'night! Pat, you comin' with us?
SUSAN. Stay.
TOM. Sure. Tony ain't gonna open an eye for a week. *(To TONY.)* 'Night, Tony.
SUSAN. Get out of here! The both of you! *(JEFFERY and TOM exit. SUSAN and PAT are alone.)* Pat...
PAT. What?
SUSAN. I've never felt so lonely in my life.
PAT. Why?
SUSAN. It has all come to this, hasn't it? All of my living and breathing... my plans, my dreams... I see my whole life coming down around me tonight. No matter what I do there's so much of it I'll never be able to change. I won't be able to change the past... and there are some things in the future I won't be able to change at all.
PAT. The future hasn't happened yet.
SUSAN. But it has. I see it happening tonight... *(SUSAN turns to PAT walking slowly toward him.)*
PAT. Sue?
SUSAN. How many strangers do we have to be intimate with before we're satisfied with what we already know?

Act II   THE ENGAGEMENT   57

PAT. Familiarity breeds contempt.
SUSAN. I'm tired of searching. I'm tried of facing the unknown everyday. I've never been so LONELY in my life!
PAT. Sue?
SUSAN. I want the familiar! I'll struggle with it!
PAT. Sue.
SUSAN. I'll hide my loneliness in you! Make love to me!
PAT. What?
SUSAN. I'll hide my loneliness in passion!
PAT. Oh, my God, Susan. *(She kisses him passionately.)*
SUSAN. I've missed you so much.
PAT. I missed you.
SUSAN. Touch me, kiss me...hold me. *(PAT returns her passionate kisses.)*
PAT. I am... I am... I am...
SUSAN. Let's make love right here...
PAT. But Tony?
SUSAN. He's asleep!
PAT. We can't...
SUSAN. I'm so...LONELY...
PAT. So am I... *(They stop.)*
SUSAN. What's wrong?
PAT. Sue... I'm losing myself...
SUSAN. That's good...
PAT. No...
SUSAN. Pat?
PAT *(steps away from SUSAN)*. It's happening...
SUSAN. What?
PAT. Feelings...deep inside me...for you...
SUSAN. Good!
PAT. No!
SUSAN. I don't understand you?

PAT. That look in your eyes...

SUSAN. What look?

PAT. You're planning my life!

SUSAN. I am not!

PAT. Look in my eyes... Look! What do you see? Tell me...

SUSAN *(looks into PAT's eyes).* Wow... You love me, don't you?

PAT. And I am planning your life. The one life you have... the one life that miraculously you've had fall into your lap... me! A perfect stranger is planning it for you!

SUSAN. I'll take the chance that the plans you have are good for me.

PAT. Don't say that, please.

SUSAN. Why?

PAT. Because I don't want the responsibility of looking into those same beautiful eyes twenty years from now wondering if you had a good life or not, because of me!

SUSAN. Don't you trust me?

PAT. Yes.

SUSAN. Don't you want me?

PAT. Yes.

SUSAN. Do you want to lose me?

PAT. No.

SUSAN. Then take a chance. We will cover one another with love just like the night under the stars in the sleeping bags.

PAT. One day we will stop seeing the stars.

SUSAN. If you don't take a chance, you'll lose me.

PAT. Can't we be friends, friends for all time? *(PAT moves around forcing a smile.)*

SUSAN. Pat?

Act II THE ENGAGEMENT 59

PAT. Friends, lovers, confidants, pals, brother and sister? We'll have adventures together! We'll share each other's hopes and ambitions!

SUSAN. Pat?

PAT. The hell with the rest of society and its rules! The hell with human nature and all of its possessiveness!

SUSAN. Pat?

PAT *(stops)*. What?

SUSAN *(with passion)*. I want to be LOVED. I need to be loved. I'm no hero. I'm no noble human being on some great quest to change the world. I want to be thought of, dreamt about, loved.

PAT. I feel that way about you.

SUSAN. If that's true, why is it every time I get close to you, you pull away?

PAT. I would love to possess you for all eternity but I haven't the skill to manipulate the pulls of gravity and old age and disappointment to even attempt such fantasy. Passion burns out.

SUSAN. I want to believe it was destiny that brought you to me and not a similar ZIP code. I want to believe that passion can be re-kindled in old age and that fate brought love to my door. *(PAT steps up to SUSAN and kisses her gently.)* What was that for?

PAT. The moment...before it becomes a memory in your mind and mine.

SUSAN. Will you run away with me?

PAT *(kisses her again gently)*. Can I think about it?

SUSAN. Think about what? When will you accept the fact that it's okay that you love me? On your deathbed when it's too late?

PAT. You're right... I know you are... I just need to think about it...

SUSAN. Think about what? My God, I am throwing my life at your feet.

PAT. I need some time.

SUSAN. You're putting me off... my passion, my needs, you can't face them!

PAT. I am going home to think... and I will call you later. *(PAT takes SUSAN confidently in his arms, holds her dearly, then kisses her with conviction.)* I will concentrate on that kiss. I want that kiss to last forever. I'll call you in the morning. I will dream of that kiss and call you when I wake up. *(PAT turns and rushes to the door.)* Alone, I can make a clear concise decision.

SUSAN. I don't want a "clear concise decision." I want YOU! *(PAT exits. She sits down at the sofa as TONY snores. Lights down.)*

SCENE TWO

SETTING: *Tony's apartment. Minutes later.*

AT RISE: *Lights up on JEFFERY and TOM facing the glow of the TV. JEFFERY is wearing his pj's.*

JEFFERY. Remember all the nights we spent here? The card games, the fantasies about the women we wanted to meet?

TOM. Yeah?

JEFFERY. I'm not good at being domestic, Tom. I can't fix anything. I hate eating at home. I don't like watching TV in the dark. I like being around people.
TOM. Hey, pal, you and me are in this for good.
JEFFERY. But, Tom?
TOM. What, Jeff?
JEFFERY. I... la... la... la... ve... her.
TOM. You what?
JEFFERY. I love... love... love... LOVE... her...
TOM. You la... lo... ve... who?
JEFFERY. H... er... errr... HER! Kim...
TOM. You... la... lo... ve... Kim?
JEFFERY. Yes.
TOM. So?
JEFFERY. I LOVE her! Shmuck!
TOM. Oh, you love Kim... LOVE? Oh, shit... you love Kim? This chick, Kim?
JEFFERY. Yes, and she loves me.
TOM. You are in more trouble then I thought.
JEFFERY. Why is this happening to me? I feel so weird inside. I feel like she's in that big city out there and I am a part of her. I feel like I am part of her shadow, her inner thoughts, her breathing, her sighs. I am inside her body totally, not even in my own! I pulsate with the same rhythm of the beating of her heart. I am beside her right this second. I am in her dreams as she sleeps. I am in the molecules of her skin, her hair, I am inside her intestines! I am part of all her bodily fluids... her insecurities... her needs! Oh, God, help me! I am in love! God, strike me dead! Paralyze me with impotence! Make me vile and disgusting! Oh, God... Oh, God... Oh, God... Tom! Where am I?

TOM *(deadpan)*. Welcome to hell. And say hello to Tony while you're there.

JEFFERY. My God, what do I do?

TOM. Pray that it goes away in twenty years.

JEFFERY. Twenty years?

TOM *(in pain himself)*. Being in love with some chick is like doing time. Once you got the sentence all you can do is serve the time. There are women in my head I still love from the first grade! Women don't know what happens to a guy when a woman's body...her soul...her voice gets into his head!

JEFFERY *(looks around the room)*. I KNOW! I see her face...everywhere I look! I see her NAME! Look, there! It's written on the wall! Look, see...K-I-M...

TOM. Take it easy...Jeff...

JEFFERY. There, look! It's on the floor...I don't believe it! K-I-M... *(Turns to TOM.)* Kill me, Tom! Buy a gun and shoot me! Kill me! *(JEFFERY falls to floor crying.)*

(PAT enters.)

PAT. What's going on?

TOM. He caught it...must had it for months and nobody knew...he did a good job of hiding it... Poor slob...

PAT. What?

TOM. He's in love.

JEFFERY. Help me fight it!

TOM. We can show her the file on you!

JEFFERY. NO! *(JEFFERY grabs the file and paces frantically.)*

PAT. The man is a goner. We should have seen it when he told us about the files. Those files are the act of a desperate man.

TOM. What do we do?

PAT. What do *I* do? Susan wants me to run away with her and I am thinking about it. *(JEFFERY walks to the phone, picks it up and dials.)*

TOM. No! Not you too! We have to stick together on this...

PAT. Is there a drug we can take? You know, wash away the memory of their faces, the way they talk?

TOM. What's he doing?

JEFFERY *(into phone)*. Hello?

TOM. Who are you calling? It's three-thirty in the morning?

JEFFERY *(into phone)*. Hello, my name is Jeffery...you will get to know about me later, I know how late it is. I'm sorry to call you now but I want you to know that I...LOVE...your wife, Kim.

TOM. Holy shit! We lost him. He went just like that. No time for surgery, nothing.

JEFFERY *(into phone)*. No, this is not a crank call. I'm an attorney. I plan to call your office in the morning but I wanted to...get this out now...while I had the courage. I will be helping your wife...Kim...get a divorce. No, don't wake her. You see, Robert, I have been seeing Kim for over a year now...and we...love each other... Yes, let's have lunch. The West Bank Cafe is nice. Their pasta is pretty good. Oh, you like Ernie's? That's fine. No, I've never been married. *(Pause.)* Thirty-three. Just never met the right girl. *(Pause.)* I'm Jewish. *(Pause.)* You sleep in separate rooms because you snore? Do I snore? I guess all men snore. She doesn't like that? I better let you get some sleep. Tell Kim... I'll call. See you at lunch. *(JEFFERY hangs up the phone.)* I don't feel well.

TOM. It's all over, pal. You're committed.

JEFFERY. Why did I do that?

TOM. It's love. You will start doing things you don't understand for the rest of your life now.

JEFFERY. I can't believe this is happening to me! I'll never get to sleep now!

TOM. No, but the guy you just woke up will be sleeping like a baby! That must have been the best call he ever had in his life! Can you imagine? There he is sleeping in the living room on the sofa because his wife doesn't like his snoring and he's lying awake trying to figure a way to get rid of her so he can spend more time with his girlfriend who doesn't complain about his snoring, yet... and in the middle of the night along comes this call from Jeffery—an answer to his prayers! I bet he picks up the check at lunch!

PAT. I bet you he lets you keep the kids, too.

JEFFERY. Kids?

TOM. She has two, doesn't she?

JEFFERY. KIDS?

TOM. I better get home and wake Denise up. I'm telling her she is moving out tomorrow.

PAT. You are going to wake her up and tell her that now?

TOM. Hey, Pat... I saw too much tonight.

PAT. You got a point. What should I do about Susan?

TOM. Do you... la... la... LOVE her?

PAT. Yes. I care about her. I have all... those feelings.

Act II   THE ENGAGEMENT   65

TOM. Fine. Then never see her again in your life. Tell yourself you can live with the thought of another man kissing her and marrying her. Jeff, you in this?

JEFFERY. Kids?

TOM. Let's you and I meet tomorrow. You stay away from Susan and I'll stay away from Denise. We make it through the night, we can make it. If you can't sleep... CALL ME! And go straight home! Swear to me!

PAT. I will go straight home. I promise.

TOM. And call me.

PAT. I will call you. The minute I get home!

TOM. I'll walk out with you. There's nothing we can do for him. *(TOM and PAT give JEFFERY one last look of pity and exit. JEFFERY rushes to the door when they leave.)*

JEFFERY. Don't leave me alone! *(Realizing he is alone, JEFFERY rushes to the file and places it in an envelope and quickly addresses it to KIM.)* To Kim Tilton, 187 Austin Street, Kew Gardens. *(He dumps his briefcase out.)* Jeffery, where are your stamps? *(JEFFERY rummages maniacally through TONY's drawers bringing out every stamp he can find.)* Tony, where are your stamps! *(He finds them.)* Yes! *(He quickly licks every stamp, stamping them all on the envelope he has addressed.)* Special Delivery! First Class! Priority Mail! Kim! Read this and weep! You think you love Jeffery? I refuse to live up to your expectations of me! Page through this and you will beg your husband to take you back! *(JEFFERY puts on his overcoat and like a man on a mission he rushes out to a mailbox.)*

(Lights up on TOM who is sitting facing a video camera in his own apartment. He turns on camera to tape.)

TOM *(facing camera)*. Denise, I am taping this for you now while you're asleep in the bedroom because I am a coward... You know I am not as tough as people think I am. You are probably the only one who knows that. So that is why I am leaving this tape for you... I want you to move out tomorrow. I will get a room at a hotel until you are out... I can't let this messy relationship go on forever... I like my freedom! You are too much of a hassle! I can live without you! *(TOM shuts off the camera.)* Oh, what the hell... *(He puts the camera back on. To camera:)* This is the truth, Denise. Why I can't see or live with you anymore. YOU GOT BORING. I mean, I come home and you're still sitting down in front of the TV. When we go out you say the same things all the time. You talk about the restaurant, your sister, your mother. You know the same people we knew when we met three years ago. You don't read any books. You don't like the movies. You don't care about my business. But that's not the way I remember you were when we first met. I remember when we talked at the party on Second Avenue that night, how exciting you looked. How interested you were in politics, sports and how you planned on going back to school. I WAS REALLY IMPRESSED. *(Pause.)* What happened to you, Denise? Once you moved in all we did was complain to each other and fight about silly things. You even lost the certain light in your eyes. The light I saw there the night I first met you. *(Pause.)* Who took that away from you? Who? I'd really like to know who changed you. Who changed you from

Act II   THE ENGAGEMENT

that exciting girl you were at the party? *(Pause.)* I'll tell you what I liked so much about you when we first met... it was that you were so DIFFERENT from me. You know I am a pretty dull guy. You know I don't like myself much. I don't like to read. I don't like the movies. I don't really like my business much. I was hoping you'd change ME and not the other way around. Wow... *(TOM shuts off the camera. He finds a note DENISE left him. Reading note:)* "Tom, wake me when you get home... no matter how late. I miss you. Love and kisses, forever and forever, Denise." Man, I can't live without you. *(TOM erases the tape and enters the bedroom. Lights out.)*

(Lights up on SUSAN and TONY. SUSAN sits on the sofa watching TONY wake up.)

TONY. Oh... man... my head... Susan? You're here? You're still here?

SUSAN. It's my apartment.

TONY. Is anybody dead? Did I kill anybody?

SUSAN. No. I am waiting for Pat to call. You can stay till he calls.

TONY. For Pat? Oh, Pat! For what? Waiting for Pat for what?

SUSAN. To let me know if we are going to run away or not. He's going to call.

TONY. He's going to call you to tell you if you two are going to run away or not?

SUSAN. Do you want some coffee?

TONY. You can't run away with him!

SUSAN. Why not?

TONY. How can you run away with a guy who has to call you to let you know if he is going to run away with you or not?

SUSAN. He has to think about it. You are his best friend!

TONY. Go ahead! Make excuses for the guy!

PAT *(offstage)*. Sue! Open up! It's me!

TONY. Open that door and I will never talk to you again!

(SUSAN rushes to the door and opens it. PAT enters stepping right up to her.)

PAT. I promised Tom I would never see you again!

TONY. You see! He's a liar, too! How can you run away with a liar?

PAT. Tony, help me! How can you say to one woman "I love you"?

TONY. Lots of concentration, pal.

SUSAN. Tony, get out of my apartment!

PAT. You walk down the street and see a woman with light brown hair! Her eyes are soft and brown and when she walks by you see this first edition copy of the *Norton Anthology of the Romantic Poets* resting in her pocket! You get this feeling you can spend all of your life just watching her sleep!

TONY *(interested)*. Outside of the reading material, let's call her Nancy.

PAT. But just then, you are hit by another woman! She's this blond, with a smile which radiates warmth in the center of a sunny day! She has just stepped into the foreign film center looking to see a revival of Fellini's *La Strada*! You would follow her face across the dark reaches of space! You want to touch her hair, suck on her toes and the street light hasn't even turned green yet!

TONY *(very interested).* That is Lisa!

SUSAN. Pat, why did you come here?

PAT. Because something drove me here! I don't have a will of my own! Because even though what happened between you and me is wrong and not fair to my friend, I don't care about that anymore. Do you understand me? When I was a kid there was this enormous billboard of a woman painted to air-brush perfection. She was smiling and looking not at me exactly but to everyone in the reaches of the universe. And I looked up at her and I said...I love you. *(With real feeling.)* I love you! *(To SUSAN.)* I LOVE YOU! And she kept smiling. *(Pause.)* I went and did it, Sue. I picked my passion for you over the friendship of my friends. Just like everybody does at least once in their lives. I don't know where this is going to lead but if I run away now I will spend the rest of my life looking for YOU in somebody else.

SUSAN. No one has ever said that to me before. *(PAT and SUSAN look deeply into each other's eyes.)*

TONY. Hey, I'm no dope. I'll go. A man has to do what a man has to do. Sue, my little Susie, right now he's the better man, but if he ever gets out of line or if you ever need anything, and I mean, anything, I am there for you, babe.

SUSAN. Thanks, Tony.

TONY. Hey, nobody can say Tony Vendome doesn't have style. My girl goes on a date and look what happens. *(TONY exits.)*

PAT. I am telling you now! I'm not going to be good at this! It may not work out. The minute I start to sound like my father or you begin to look like my mother to me...I mean, the minute I have to walk out of my own house to get some air to feel free and complete—I will get in my car and never turn back.

SUSAN. The day that happens will be the day after I already left.

PAT. I don't want you to leave. I want you to stay forever.

SUSAN. Those were my plans, too.

PAT. Just remember—there are a lot of things we are going to have to analyze and figure out. It's going to take a lot of work! You got that?

SUSAN. Pat, come here. Let's take a chance and see what happens.

PAT *(big smile)*. Yeah. *(They embrace. Lights slowly down.)*

(Lights up on TONY who enters his apartment and takes off his jacket. He mixes himself a drink opening his phone book looking at the names and numbers.)

TONY. Let's see...Barbara...not back until next week. Lisa... Lisa?.. *(Checks watch.)* Four a.m.? *(TONY dials the number and speaks into the phone).* Lisa? *(TONY sings into phone.)* "When a man loves a woman..." *(Lights out on TONY.)*

(Lights up on JEFFERY who is standing at a mailbox dressed in his raincoat and slippers. He drops the file into the mailbox. Thunder explodes above.)

JEFFERY. I did it! I did it! *(Pause.)* Why the hell did I do it? I have to get it back! *(JEFFERY reaches down into the mailbox desperately trying to get back the file. Sud-*

denly it begins to downpour on JEFFERY.) She'll read it and she'll hate me! *(JEFFERY pulls out his cellular phone and dials Kim's number in the rain. Into phone:)* Robert! It's me, Jeffery! Wake her! Please, for God's sake, wake her! *(Pause.)* Kim? Oh, Kim! I know what time it is! You will be getting a package in the mail! It's a FILE... DO NOT OPEN IT! Some creep put it together! I love you! Do you hear me? I LOVE YOU! *(Lights out.)*

END OF PLAY

ADDITIONAL CHARACTER NOTES

PAT: A life-long friend of Tony's, he went to college to study English Literature. Single, he is unassuming, well-read with a fondness for romantic literature. He is articulate, sensitive and like many educated people—he is analytical and indecisive. He wears a herringbone jacket, and a shirt and tie.

JEFFERY: Knows Pat from college. Single and petrified of love, he volunteers his practical knowledge to the group of guys. He wears a conservative suit and is never without his briefcase.

TOM: Another life-long friend of Tony's, he is from a blue-collar family in Queens and has a rough edge to him. A hard player in the night life, he was a bartender who invested in a rock club before becoming owner of one of the most successful nightclubs in the city. Inundated with young women and money, he is a bachelor who has had to hold onto his dated, macho attitude to survive.

SUSAN: She is pretty but not in a glamorous way. From the "neighborhood," she wanted to do something with her life after high school so she traveled. Though she didn't go to college, she is self-taught and loves to read. Not sure what to do with her life, she wanted to be an actress, but now, she designs textbook covers part-time as well as working for Tony for the last two years. She dresses as her finances can afford: stylish and hip but still womanly and feminine.

TONY: Born and raised in Queens, he is single, handsome, energetic, and narcissistic. He knows the words to every pop love song ever made and is in love with love which helps him justify to himself, his out-and-out womanizing. A contemporary Byronic-hero. He is dressed in a dark, expensive suit.